Original title:
Frosted Shadows

Copyright © 2024 Swan Charm
All rights reserved.

Author: Linda Leevike
ISBN HARDBACK: 978-9916-79-585-9
ISBN PAPERBACK: 978-9916-79-586-6
ISBN EBOOK: 978-9916-79-587-3

Eclipsed by Winter's Charm

Snowflakes dance like whispers soft,
Frosted trees in silence loft.
Moonlight glints on frozen streams,
Winter weaves its silver dreams.

Heartbeats quicken with the chill,
Morning glows on distant hill.
A world transformed in icy breath,
Where time holds fast, seduced by death.

Footsteps crunch on snowy ground,
Echoes of the wild surround.
Nature's splendor, cold and bright,
Eclipsed beneath the velvet night.

Whispers of a winter's tale,
In the hush, we hear the gale.
Stars adorned in crystal lace,
Winter's charm, a quiet grace.

A Palette of Frozen Echoes

Colors blend in icy streams,
Pastel hues like faded dreams.
Blue and white, a canvas pure,
Nature's art, both bold and sure.

Mountains rise with caps of snow,
Silent witnesses to glow.
Echoes of the past reside,
In this realm where fears subside.

Sunset hues, a fleeting glance,
Reflections caught in twilight dance.
Whispers soft as shadows creep,
In winter's hold, the world's asleep.

Brushstrokes glide with gentle grace,
Every corner, a hidden space.
Frigid air holds mysteries deep,
In a palette where echoes weep.

Beneath the Glacial Sky

Stars peer down from velvet night,
Beneath their watchful, icy light.
A crystal dome encases dreams,
Where silence reigns, and beauty gleams.

The night unfolds its chilly wing,
On frozen fields, the shadows cling.
Footsteps wander, hearts entwined,
In hushed whispers, fate aligned.

Glistening frost on every leaf,
Moments dance, a quiet thief.
Underneath this frozen sphere,
Lies a world both far and near.

Gaze upwards, seek the divine,
In the frost, star light will shine.
Beneath the glacial sky we stand,
In the stillness, hand in hand.

Where Shadows and Ice Converge

Silhouettes in twilight glow,
Where shadows stretch, and cold winds blow.
Ice-bound branches weave and sway,
In the dance of night and day.

Fractured light on frozen ground,
In this realm, no warmth is found.
Chill embraces every breath,
In a landscape chest-deep in death.

Rivulets of silvered flow,
Where ancient whispers softly go.
The world asleep, a canvas stark,
Where shadows dwell, and dreams embark.

Each step echoes through the night,
In the stillness, find the light.
Between the shadows and the frost,
Life's memory is never lost.

Glistening Murmurs of the Solstice

Whispers dance upon the breeze,
A gentle call among the trees.
Stars awaken, shimmering bright,
Guiding hearts through the night.

Moonlit paths in silver glow,
Softly tracing where we go.
In this magic, time stands still,
Echoes linger, sweet and shrill.

Glistening dreams unfold their wings,
Nature's song of countless things.
Together under cosmic sky,
We find the moments drifting by.

Joyous laughter fills the air,
Solstice magic everywhere.
With each murmur, secrets twine,
In our hearts, forever shine.

Shadows Beneath the Silvered Sky

In twilight's hush, the world unfolds,
Shadows stretch as daylight holds.
Whispers brush against the night,
Softly stealing all the light.

Beneath the silvered sky we roam,
Finding solace, feeling home.
Every corner hides a tale,
In the darkness, dreams set sail.

Glimmers dance in fleeting glances,
Serenade of soft romances.
Heartbeats echo, pulses rise,
In the depths where silence lies.

Every step a secret shared,
In this stillness, hearts laid bare.
Together in the shadowed glow,
Life's true essence starts to flow.

The Quiet Embrace of Winter's Breath

Frosty whispers fill the air,
Nature shivers, calm and rare.
Blankets white beneath the trees,
Stillness comes on whispered breeze.

Footprints mark a cold terrain,
Echoes of the softest rain.
In this chill, we find our peace,
Winter's hug, a sweet release.

Stars are sharp against the night,
In their glow, we feel the light.
Each breath visible like a cloud,
Silence wraps us, soft and loud.

With every flake that gently falls,
Magic dances, softly calls.
In the quiet, warmth we weave,
In winter's grasp, we learn to believe.

Shimmering Frost upon Forgotten Paths

Morning breaks with muted hues,
Frosty petals, whispered clues.
Hidden trails wake from their sleep,
Secrets buried, still and deep.

Glistening leaves, a jeweled thread,
Where every step the ancients tread.
Nature's canvas, tranquil, bright,
Guides us forth into the light.

Through the fog, our spirits roam,
Finding beauty in the loam.
Every path that once was lost,
Now shines bright, no matter the cost.

With each breath, the world unfolds,
In the silence, magic holds.
Shimmering frost, a gentle kiss,
On forgotten paths, we find bliss.

Twilit Secrets of the Frosty Woods

Whispers ride the evening breeze,
Where shadows dance on trembling trees.
Secrets hide in frosty air,
Nature's breath, a lingering prayer.

Moonlight spills on silver streams,
Echoing ancient woodland dreams.
In the hush, a moment stays,
Time descends in quiet ways.

Footfalls soft on snowbitten ground,
Lost in a world where peace is found.
Branches weave a tapestry bright,
Twilit secrets come to light.

Every glance, a hidden truth,
Starlit eyes reclaiming youth.
In the woods, where shadows play,
Twilit secrets softly sway.

Amidst the chill, a warmth unfolds,
Stories whispered, whispered old.
Wrapped in nature's quiet fold,
Twilit secrets, brave and bold.

Lurking in the Glistening Gloom

Fog creeps low on the forest floor,
Cloaking all, open the door.
Shadows shift, as night descends,
Whispers rise, as daylight ends.

Glistening eyes in the dark await,
Lurking figures, tempting fate.
Mysterious forms in the silvery mist,
Calling softly, you can't resist.

Underneath the boughs they hide,
Lost in magic, dreams abide.
Dancing lightly on the air,
Every heartbeat, a silent prayer.

Tangled roots and soft-spun tales,
Furtive sighs on midnight trails.
Nature holds her secrets tight,
Lurking in the glistening night.

As the stars begin to gleam,
Faded wishes, half a dream.
In the gloom, the shadows creep,
Lurking echoes never sleep.

Shades of Crystal Light

Fragments of dawn on emerald leaves,
Whispering breezes through ancient eaves.
Nature's canvas, soft and bright,
Emerge with shades of crystal light.

Icicles dangle, prismed glow,
Painting rainbows in winter's show.
Every drop a glowing sight,
A symphony of pure delight.

Gentle rays kiss the frosted ground,
Magic weaves all around.
In the stillness, joy ignites,
Wrapped in shades of crystal light.

Misty fog, a silken shroud,
Yet beneath it, nature's proud.
Every moment feels just right,
Bringing forth shades, crystal bright.

As daylight fades, colors fade too,
Silhouettes dance 'neath skies of blue.
In every hue, a strong invite,
To cherish shades of crystal light.

The Enchantment of the Cold Moon

Cold moon hangs in velvet skies,
Casting dreams with luminous eyes.
Whispers float on silver beams,
Eclipsed in night, my spirit dreams.

Glimmers shine on the frozen ground,
Echoing night in a sonorous sound.
In the dark, the heart takes flight,
Ensnared by the cold moon's light.

Boughs adorned in glistening frost,
Nature's grace, never lost.
Each sigh, a sweet delight,
Lost forever in the night.

Secrets linger, sweet yet bold,
In the warmth, it feels so cold.
Breathless beauty, pure and right,
In the spell of the cold moonlight.

Flakes of snow like glitter fall,
Echoing peace, a gentle call.
In its glow, our hearts unite,
Drawn into the cold moon's light.

Serenity of the Icebound Hour

In the hush of twilight's grace,
Winter's breath, a soft embrace,
Silence whispers through the trees,
Frozen stillness, hearts at ease.

Stars awaken, twinkle bright,
Guiding dreams in tranquil night,
Shadows dancing, softly sway,
In the calm, we find our way.

Crystal pathways, glisten cold,
Stories of the brave and bold,
Every flake, a tale to share,
In the ice, a world laid bare.

Eagles soar in skies so wide,
Nature's canvas, pure and white,
Peaceful visions, hearts align,
In the stillness, we define.

Moments fleeting, yet divine,
In this hour, we intertwine,
Breath of winter, soft and low,
Serenity begins to flow.

Shimmers in the Pale Moonlight

Beneath the glow of silver beams,
Whispers dance like fleeting dreams,
Fingers trace the gentle night,
Shadows glisten, pure delight.

The world is bathed in soft embrace,
As stars twinkle, find their place,
Every moment feels so rare,
In this magic, we lay bare.

Nightingale sings a tender song,
In this harmony, we belong,
Velvet skies, a deepened hue,
Moonlit wonders, a world anew.

Glances shared, so tender, true,
In the stillness, just us two,
Hand in hand, we wander slow,
In pale moonlight's calming glow.

Memories captured in the light,
Fleeting visions, pure delight,
In this tranquil, fleeting trance,
Here's our moment, take a chance.

Frost-Kissed Reveries of the Night

Frosted whispers on the ground,
Echoing in silence found,
Stars above with tales untold,
In the night, our dreams unfold.

Snowflakes twirl like dancers fair,
Painting secrets in the air,
Blanket soft on slumber deep,
Wrapped in warmth, we fall asleep.

Glistening paths of silver trails,
Nature sings as winter pales,
Every breath, a crystal sigh,
Underneath the vast, dark sky.

Harmonies of night shall play,
Guiding hearts along the way,
With each beat, we feel alive,
In this magic, we survive.

Echoes linger, memories breathe,
In the frost, our dreams believe,
Cherished moments, soft yet bright,
In frost-kissed reveries of night.

Whispers Beneath a Blanket of Snow

A hush descends, the world at peace,
Whispers fade, the moments cease,
Blanket white, embracing all,
In winter's grace, we softly fall.

Gentle flakes, a tender shroud,
Cradled dreams beneath the cloud,
Nature sighs in soft repose,
In this wonder, beauty grows.

Fires crackle, warmth surrounds,
Among the trees, the silence sounds,
Footsteps echo, soft and slow,
In the stillness, love will flow.

Stars in silence watch above,
Guiding hearts that seek for love,
In this realm, the world unites,
Whispers shared on snowy nights.

Memories linger, soft and bright,
Underneath the starlit night,
In each flake, a secret told,
Beneath the snow, our hearts unfold.

Ethereal Twilight Glimmer

In the hush of twilight's breeze,
Stars awaken, dance with ease.
Softly whispers the fading light,
Painting shadows, day to night.

Gentle hues of purple and gold,
Secrets of the skies unfold.
A fleeting moment, beauty rare,
Ethereal echoes fill the air.

As day gives way, dreams take flight,
In the soft embrace of night.
Glimmers twinkle, hopes arise,
In the depth of starlit skies.

Silent wishes, hearts entwined,
In the dusk, solace we find.
Underneath the cosmic dome,
We wander through the twilight home.

In this realm where time stands still,
Filled with wonder, grace, and thrill.
Ethereal moments, pure delight,
Carried softly on the night.

Fragments of a Frozen Dream

In the quiet of a winter's breath,
Lies a world untouched by death.
Crystal shards of dreams so bright,
Dancing softly in the light.

Misty visions in the cold,
Whispers lost, stories told.
Each flake falls with gentle grace,
Embracing beauty in its place.

A dreamscape woven, pure and deep,
In silver silence, secrets sleep.
Branches draped in frosted lace,
Nature's art, a tranquil space.

Time stands still in this serene,
A fleeting glimpse of what has been.
Lost in wonder, we explore,
Fragments whispering evermore.

Awakened hearts beneath the sky,
In frozen dreams, we soar and fly.
Through the chill, we find our way,
In the light of a winter's day.

Veiled Glades of Winter's Breath

Hidden glades where silence reigns,
Whispers float like gentle chains.
Underneath a blanket white,
Nature holds her breath at night.

Branches bowed with softest snow,
Veils of ice in moonlit glow.
Secrets shrouded, shadows beckon,
In these woods, memories reckon.

Echoes linger, time stands still,
In the quiet, hearts can fill.
Mysteries in every fold,
Veiled glades telling stories old.

Each step taken, crisp and clear,
Winter's breath is always near.
Through the chill, a warmth we find,
In the depths of nature's mind.

Underneath the starry sky,
We wander where the wild things lie.
In this sanctuary, so profound,
Veiled glades whisper joy unbound.

Echoes of the Icy Moon

In the night where shadows loom,
Lingers softly the icy moon.
Casting light on frozen streams,
Illuminating whispered dreams.

A glow that paints the world anew,
Silver beams in shades of blue.
Through the dark, a path we trace,
Finding warmth in moon's embrace.

Echoes dance upon the snow,
Songs of secrets carried low.
In this stillness, magic brews,
Underneath the moonlit hues.

Each heartbeat echoes through the night,
In the presence of pale light.
Guiding souls lost in despair,
To a place where dreams repair.

And as the world turns, we behold,
Stories whispered, tales retold.
In the quiet, shadows swoon,
Bound forever by the moon.

Frost-tinged Memories of Yesterday

In the silver glow of dawn,
Whispers of dreams still remain,
Each crystal breathes a song,
Of moments lost, but not in vain.

Footprints fade in the sparkling white,
Echoes of laughter fill the air,
Chasing shadows, hearts take flight,
In a world woven with care.

Frosted branches, stories told,
Beneath the boughs of a frosty tree,
Every memory, a shard of gold,
Captured in time, forever free.

The chill wraps round like a gentle embrace,
Every flake, a memory's kiss,
Winter holds them in a delicate space,
A tapestry of cold, love, and bliss.

As twilight fades to the starry night,
Those frost-tinged moments linger near,
In the heart, they shine so bright,
A timeless warmth that draws us here.

Shadows Beneath the Icicles

Hanging in silence, the icicles gleam,
Shadows dance on the moonlit ground,
Nature whispers, weaving a dream,
With frost and cold, all around.

A crackling fire, warmth and light,
Flickering thoughts, lost in the night,
Beneath the mantle of icy air,
Shadows sway, as if aware.

Branches bow with a chill so deep,
Whispers echo through the forest bare,
In winter's grasp, the world is asleep,
With secrets fluttering in the air.

Yet in the dark, a glow ignites,
Hope flickers under starlit skies,
Shadows linger, revealing sights,
Where dreams awaken, softly arise.

As dawn approaches, cold turns to gray,
Icicles melt, their forms unspun,
Yet shadows remain, just a heartbeat away,
Echoes of winter, a race just begun.

The Frigid Palette of the Dusk

Colors collide in the twilight gloom,
A frigid palette brushes the air,
Pink and blue in a cold costume,
Winter's breath, a painter rare.

The sun dips low, a final embrace,
Casting shadows, long and deep,
Every hue holds a fleeting grace,
In the stillness, secrets keep.

Silhouettes dance on the snowy field,
Woven threads of light and cold,
Nature's canvas, forever healed,
In silent moments, stories unfold.

Underneath the fading light,
A chill wraps round like an unseen crest,
The frigid palette, a tranquil sight,
A world paused, in quiet rest.

As night descends, the colors blend,
Stars emerge, a glittering map,
With each whisper, winter lends,
A beauty caught in nature's lap.

Ephemeral Threads of Winter's Breath

In fragile webs spun of ice,
Winter's breath, a fleeting thread,
Glittering softly, so precise,
Binding dreams, where none dare tread.

Each frost-kissed moment fades away,
Elusive as the morning dew,
Yet in their chill, memories stay,
Whispering tales known by few.

Snowflakes fall with a gentle grace,
Each one different, a work of art,
In winter's tapestry, they find their place,
Warming the corners of a cold heart.

Embracing the silence, we stand so still,
Listening close to the world beyond,
Ephemeral threads weave a quiet thrill,
In winter's cradle, souls are fond.

As seasons shift and timelines blur,
The breath of winter lingers here,
In every flake, a gentle stir,
A reminder of love, forever near.

Shattered Dreams in a Winter Frame

Frosted whispers touch the air,
Once bright hopes now cold and bare.
Mirrors crack with silent screams,
In the heart, lie shattered dreams.

Blankets of snow catch the light,
Memories fade, lost in the night.
Each flake falls, a past untold,
Fractured stories, hearts turned cold.

Winds howl through the barren trees,
Echoes of what used to be.
Yet in the quiet, silence speaks,
Healing the wounds, though hope feels weak.

Each star shines through the endless grey,
A promise that light will find a way.
In winter's arms, dreams must rest,
Awaiting spring to bring their best.

Light Within the Frigid Maze

In a world wrapped in icy chains,
Where shadows dance, and silence reigns.
Hope flickers like a candle's thread,
Guiding lost souls, where all seems dead.

Winding paths of glistening white,
Twisting, turning, lost from sight.
Yet deep within, a warmth ignites,
A spark of joy that gently fights.

Voices linger in the crisp air,
Echoes of dreams that once were fair.
Through the maze, the heart must roam,
Finding in darkness, a way back home.

Amidst the cold, the spirit thrives,
In winter's clutch, the heart survives.
For every turn brings hope anew,
A light awaits, the path to view.

Shadows Painted on the White Canvas

Upon the snow, the shadows fall,
Silent stories whisper and call.
Footprints left by wanderers near,
Marking moments, joy and fear.

Each shadow tells of dreams once bright,
Now cloaked in the fading light.
They dance and sway with the winter's breeze,
Fleeting forms that aim to please.

What colors blend in this quiet place,
A canvas touched with nature's grace?
Painting memories in shades of grey,
Yet beauty lies in the shades of play.

In every swirl, a tale unfolds,
Of love, of loss, of dreams retold.
In winter's freeze, the heart must feel,
These painted shadows, so surreal.

The Allure of Cold Radiance

In the midnight sky, stars align,
A glimmer of hope, a promise divine.
Frozen lakes reflect the night,
Capturing cold in silver light.

The allure of frost, a tempting touch,
Each crystalline form, beckons so much.
Nature's beauty draped in white,
A silent majesty, pure delight.

Even in chill, hearts can ignite,
Finding warmth in the serene sight.
The beauty of ice, sharp yet fair,
A paradox, to dream and dare.

As dawn breaks through the winter haze,
The world awakens, lost in a daze.
Yet in the cold, a fire we chase,
In the heart's warmth, we find our place.

Threnody for a Winter's Night

The cold winds wail a chilling tune,
Underneath the silver moon.
Whispers float through the barren trees,
Carried softly on frozen breeze.

Shadows dance on glimmering snow,
Where quiet tales of sorrow flow.
Stars twinkle with a distant glow,
Marking time as the night moves slow.

Footprints lost in a hush profound,
Echoes linger, making no sound.
Lost dreams drift in the icy air,
A haunting pulse, a whispered prayer.

The hearth burns low, a flickering flame,
Yet the heart remains wild and untame.
In solitude, we face our plight,
A threnody for the winter's night.

Each breath is mist, each thought a sigh,
As memories fade like clouds in the sky.
Wrapping shadows close as we part,
A lament played on the strings of the heart.

The Enigma of Glacial Metaphors

Frozen thoughts like shards of glass,
Reflecting truths that slowly pass.
Words encased in crystalline hue,
Reveal the layers that time withdrew.

A mountain's secret, draped in ice,
Holds echoes of a steep sacrifice.
Metaphors chill, yet warmly tease,
The frozen tongue of winter's freeze.

In silence whispered by ancient trees,
Life's enigmas ride the winter's breeze.
Each flake a story, delicate, rare,
A fleeting glimpse of the world laid bare.

A tapestry of frost unfolds,
Mysteries in the chill it holds.
As glaciers move with ancient grace,
Time unveils its hidden place.

To wander through these frozen dreams,
Is to seek the truth in silver beams.
Beneath each layer, wisdom grows,
In the glacial metaphors we propose.

Dappled Light Upon Frosted Terrain

Morning breaks with gentle light,
Dancing softly, banishing night.
Frosted veins on the ground do glisten,
In this beauty, the heart can't help but listen.

The trees wear coats of sparkling white,
Naked branches in pure delight.
Nature's canvas, a painter's dream,
Each ray of sunshine starts to beam.

Footprints trace where wanderers roam,
In the midst of this crystal dome.
The quiet whispers of dawn's embrace,
Dappled light finds its rightful place.

Birds take flight in arcs of grace,
Painting shadows in a hurried race.
Chirps entwined with the golden sun,
A symphony of life has begun.

In through the frost, the warmth does creep,
Awakening spirits from their sleep.
Upon this terrain, beauty reigns,
A world adorned with soft refrains.

Frost's Muffled Secrets in the Dark

In the stillness, winter's breath,
Holds the echoes of silent death.
Secrets wrapped in a chilly shroud,
Whispers buried beneath the crowd.

Frosty tendrils grip the night,
Veiling mysteries from the light.
Each flake a guardian of the past,
Stories hidden, shadows cast.

The moon hangs low, a watchful eye,
Surveying earth with a knowing sigh.
Yet in the dark, truths come alive,
As the quiet night begins to thrive.

Velvet silence wraps the trees,
Cradling hopes in the icy freeze.
Hidden whispers, a nature's art,
Frost's soft secrets, held close to heart.

Unraveled thoughts with morning's dew,
Awake the dreams we once knew.
In this dark, stillness calls,
Frost's muffled secrets, through twilight falls.

Chilling Elegy of Silent Nights

In the quiet of the night, still and deep,
The stars whisper secrets that shadows keep.
Moonlight drapes softly, a silken sheet,
On dreams that linger, both bitter and sweet.

A breeze kisses softly, a spectral sigh,
Caressing the edges where once laughter lay.
Memories dance in the cold, pale glow,
In the silence, a story unfolds so slow.

Frost adorns the windows, a crystal lace,
Each flake a reminder of time's swift pace.
Echoes of voices long forgotten float,
In the chill of the night, we feel their hope.

A heartbeat of solitude fills the air,
Wrapped in the stillness, we burden our care.
Yearning for warmth in the frostbitten silence,
In chilling elegy, we find our reliance.

Through the inky shadows, lost souls weep,
For the warmth of their laughter, a promise to keep.
Yet in the darkness, a flicker remains,
Of a comforting love that endures our pains.

Glimmering Frost on Bare Branches

In the dawn's soft light, whispers of white,
Glimmering frost paints the world with delight.
Bare branches shimmer like dancers in trance,
Each crystal a story, a fleeting romance.

A silent enchantment, where silence reigns,
Nature's poetry woven through brittle veins.
Every breath icy, each moment a pause,
Celebrating beauty, the winter's applause.

As sunlight kisses the frost with a glow,
Shadows recede, colors start to flow.
A canvas of silver, so serene and bright,
In this winter wonder, all feels just right.

Beneath the cold splendor, warmth still hides,
In the hearts of the trees, where tenderness bides.
A reminder of life, in stark contrast stands,
Glimmering frost, cradled in nature's hands.

When dusk wraps the world in a velvet sigh,
The frost becomes radiant, beneath the sky.
As stars blink awake, the night draws near,
In the twinkling silence, our dreams appear.

Ethereal Twilight in Silver Hues

As day surrenders to night's soft embrace,
Ethereal twilight adorns every space.
Silver hues shimmer upon the cool air,
A moment of magic, both fragile and rare.

Veils of dusk whisper sweet tales in light,
Painting the horizon in shades of delight.
With each fading breath of the sun's warm glow,
Night cradles the world in a gentle shadow.

Stars begin twinkling, their secrets unfold,
A tapestry woven with threads of pure gold.
In this tranquil hour, all worries subside,
As we dance with the dreams that the twilight provides.

The moon peeks softly from behind the clouds,
Wrapping the earth in its silvery shrouds.
Each heartbeat resonates with nature's refrain,
In a world cloaked in serenity, hope reigns.

With every star's flicker, a wish is cast,
In this ethereal moment, we've found our past.
In the stillness of twilight, we linger anew,
Cradled by silence, wrapped in silver hues.

Specters of the Icebound Forest

Through the mist of the evening, shadows arise,
Specters of old wrapped in secrets and sighs.
The forest stands still, encased in a chill,
Where whispers of dreams fade, but linger still.

Beneath icy boughs, a silence profound,
Footsteps of phantoms echo all around.
Once vibrant with life, now hushed and restrained,\nIn the grip of the frost, all warmth is gamed.

Each tree a sentinel, ancient and wise,
Holding the stories that the winter despise.
Frosted branches reaching, like fingers to touch,
The remnants of memories that linger so much.

In the heart of the cold, a flicker of grace,
In shadows long woven, we all find our place.
Lost in the whispers that dance in the night,
The specters remind us of beauty and light.

So tread soft and low in this kingdom of frost,
Where the tales of the past remind us what's lost.
In the heart of the forest, where time seems to fade,
Specters of the icebound, in silence we wade.

Whispering Shadows of Frost

In the hush of night, frost takes flight,
Whispers of silence, under moonlight.
Crystals shimmer, on branches bare,
Beneath the stars, a chilling air.

Softly they dance, through the trees,
Nature's breath, carried by the breeze.
Each gleam a story, of winter told,
Secrets slumber, in the cold.

Echoes linger, in the frosty mist,
Promises kept, in twilight kissed.
The world asleep, in this frozen hour,
Beauty captured, in icy power.

Time stands still, in a glistening shroud,
Wrapped in wonder, nature's proud.
Whispers and shadows, in perfect form,
Embracing the silence, of the storm.

A path adorned, with glacial lace,
Guides the weary, through this grace.
Gentle touches, of winter's art,
Whispering shadows, in every heart.

Secrets Veiled in Icy Light

Upon the lake, a mirror gleams,
Veiled in frost, where daylight beams.
Hidden wonders, beneath the skin,
Secrets whisper, where dreams begin.

A delicate weave, of ice and snow,
Nature's canvas, a silent show.
The world enchained, in crystal bonds,
Echoes of magic, of silent fronds.

Moonlight dances, on silver streams,
Unveiling stories, of winter's dreams.
Each glimmered spark, a tale unfolds,
In whispered tones, the night beholds.

Softly it fades, as dawn breaks near,
Unveiling truths, once draped in fear.
Icy light reveals, what shadows hide,
Secrets borne, on the winter tide.

In the stillness, winter's breath,
Lives in whispers, beyond the death.
Each frost-kissed moment, a fleeting art,
Veiled in ice, yet close to the heart.

A Solstice's Frozen Dream

Beneath the stars, winter's embrace,
A frozen dream, in this still place.
Time suspends, in the solstice night,
Whispers carried, on soft moonlight.

Paths of silver, through woods so deep,
Where ancient memories, silently sleep.
Cloaked in white, the world at rest,
Nature's heart, in slumber dressed.

Each breath a cloud, in the frigid air,
Dreams weave softly, without a care.
The flicker of lights, in distance seen,
Echoing tales, of once and been.

A promise made, in the frozen glow,
Of warmer days, that we may know.
Yet in this chill, a magic swirls,
In the frost-kissed verses, the cosmos twirls.

Awake in wonder, hear the call,
In the depth of winter, we find it all.
A solstice dream, in radiant night,
Forever cherished, in heart's delight.

Shadows of the Icy Canopy

Under the boughs, where silence reigns,
Shadows linger, in frozen chains.
Icy tendrils, grasp at the light,
A world transformed, in winter's bite.

The canopy glistens, each branch a star,
Whispers of secrets, from afar.
Snowflakes gather, upon the ground,
In this quiet place, peace is found.

Footsteps muffled, in powdery white,
Leading us deeper, into the night.
With each breath taken, the frosty air,
Wraps around us, in tender care.

A tapestry woven, of ice and sky,
In shadows dancing, as time drifts by.
Nature's artistry, on full display,
In the icy canopy, we lose our way.

Yet in this lost, enchanting maze,
We find our hearts, in winter's gaze.
For in each shadow, a story lives,
Of moments captured, that winter gives.

Enshrined in Winter's Glow

In the quiet of the night,
Stars shimmer, cold and bright,
Blankets soft, the world asleep,
Winter's secrets, ours to keep.

Whispers break the silent air,
Snowflakes drift without a care,
Each a tale, each a dream,
Beneath the moon's soft beam.

Frosty branches gently sway,
In the hush, we feel the play,
Nature wrapped in purest white,
Enshrined in winter's light.

Footsteps muffled in the snow,
Silent paths where we will go,
Holding hands, our breath a mist,
In this scene, we can't resist.

Time stands still, our hearts align,
Underneath that starry sign,
Wrapped in warmth, we find our way,
Enshrined in winter's sway.

The Hushed Dance of Snowflakes

In a world of white so deep,
Snowflakes twirl, drift, and leap,
Each a feather, light and rare,
Whirling softly through the air.

Frosty whispers fill the night,
Silent beauty, pure delight,
A gentle waltz, a twinkling show,
The magic of the falling snow.

Every flake with stories spun,
Unique patterns, all in fun,
In their dance, a silent song,
Inviting hearts to join along.

Underneath the moon's soft gaze,
Snowflakes shimmer, lost in praise,
A ballet on the winter ground,
Joyful whispers all around.

As they settle, dreams arise,
Cloaked in peace, beneath the skies,
The world transformed, a frozen grace,
In winter's hush, we find our place.

Glistening Wounds of a Silent Night

The moonlight drapes the quiet scene,
Over shadows, soft and lean,
Stars like sapphires cut the dark,
A sharp beauty, a sudden spark.

In the stillness, sorrow weaves,
Whispers linger upon the leaves,
Echoes of a heart's deep sigh,
Glistening wounds beneath the sky.

Cold winds carry tales of pain,
Memories of love like rain,
Each drop, a wound that glows so bright,
Illuminating the silent night.

Yet in the darkness, hope will grow,
Healing under the soft snow,
A quiet strength, a gentle light,
Glistening through the longest night.

As dawn approaches, shadows fade,
Renewed paths from wounds that stayed,
In the silence, we find grace,
Glistening memories we embrace.

Echoes of Glimmering Stillness

In the calm of twilight's breath,
Lies the magic born of death,
Silent echoes float and gleam,
Through the night, a tender dream.

Stillness blankets every place,
Time suspended, a warm embrace,
In the air, a gentle chill,
Whispers linger, hearts to fill.

Glimmers dance on frosted pane,
Beautiful, yet laced with pain,
In this peace, the world stands still,
Echoes soft, a quiet thrill.

Each moment a treasure to hold,
Stories told and loosely sold,
Captured in the night's soft hue,
Glimmering, the past shines through.

As dawn approaches, dreams take flight,
The heart awakens to the light,
In stillness, echoes softly call,
To embrace the beauty of it all.

Secrets Wrapped in Winter's Embrace

Whispers float on icy air,
Silent tales of love laid bare.
Carried softly through the trees,
Frozen echoes on the breeze.

Crystals blanket every ground,
In their stillness, dreams are found.
Softly sparkling, night's delight,
Wrapped in cozy, soft twilight.

Fires flicker in the glow,
Stories told of long ago.
As the world holds its breath tight,
Secrets linger in the night.

Footsteps crunch on frosty trails,
Each one tells of hidden tales.
In the shadows, deep and wide,
Winter's heart, a place to hide.

Every flake, a story spun,
In the moonlight, two become one.
Embers warm the chill outside,
In this season, hearts confide.

Nightfall's Frigid Caress

Underneath the starry skies,
Moonlight twinkles, softly lies.
Cold winds whisper through the night,
Cradled in their gentle bite.

Barren branches, stark and bare,
Reach for dreams that linger there.
Each shadow speaks of what's to come,
In the silence, hearts are numb.

Frosty patterns grace each pane,
Nature's art, both fierce and plain.
Latent hopes like snowflakes fall,
Frigid air cloaks one and all.

In the stillness, secrets dwell,
Wrapped in winter's frozen spell.
Nightfall's caress, a fleeting sight,
Holds the warmth of hidden light.

As the world lies still and deep,
Dreams weave softly, whispering sleep.
In the darkness, futures spin,
In night's embrace, we begin.

Reflection in the Icy Silence

Glimmers dance on frozen lakes,
Mirrored dreams and gentle shakes.
In the quiet, thoughts align,
Nature's canvas, pure design.

Frosted edges, beauty rare,
Stillness hints at hidden care.
Every glance a world defined,
In this peace, our hearts entwined.

Footsteps echo, soft and slow,
Breaking through the crystal glow.
In the silence, voices blend,
Winter's breath, a loyal friend.

Ripples form as hearts reflect,
The frozen world, a perfect sketch.
In each pause, a breath we take,
For in stillness, dreams awake.

Hushed confessions, softly shared,
In icy silence, none are scared.
As the dusk brings forth its grace,
Find your truth in winter's face.

A Dance of Shimmering Snow

Snowflakes twirl in frozen air,
Casting magic everywhere.
In the glow of twilight's beam,
Nature's whispers start to dream.

Glistening under pale moonlight,
Each flake brings its pure delight.
Winter's waltz, a soft refrains,
In the night, they dance like chains.

Barefoot footprints in the white,
Leading to a world of light.
Children laugh and play and spin,
Lost in joy where dreams begin.

Branches sway, the winds comply,
Nature's serenade is nigh.
With each step, the rhythm grows,
In sweet harmony, the snow flows.

As the dawn breaks, visions fade,
Yet in hearts, the dance is made.
With every flake that falls anew,
Winter's spirit, pure and true.

Twinkling Eyes of the Frozen Forest

In the woods where shadows creep,
Twinkling eyes awaken sleep.
Whispers dance on icy air,
Secrets hidden, yet laid bare.

Frosted branches rise so tall,
Nature's magic weaves a thrall.
Silent watch from boughs above,
Guardians of the wild, they love.

Moonlight kisses frozen streams,
While the night unravels dreams.
Eternal tale of life and loss,
Underneath the winter's gloss.

Footsteps muffled, soft and light,
In this realm of silver night.
With each step, the world unfolds,
Stories of the brave and bold.

Stars align in vast expanse,
Inviting hearts to take a chance.
Embracing all the magic here,
In the forest, calm and clear.

Embrace of the Chilling Veil

Wrapped in fog, a soft embrace,
Whispers linger, time and place.
Cold and warmth begin to blend,
Where the silence seems to mend.

Hushed are dreams that softly tread,
Beneath the snow-clad heavens spread.
Frosty tendrils twist and weave,
In this realm, we let believe.

Shadows flicker, fleeting light,
In the depth of winter's night.
Every breath, a crystal shard,
In the stillness, we feel scarred.

The chilling veil begins to sway,
As dawn breaks upon the day.
Nature's beauty, fierce and bold,
Encapsulating tales untold.

Gentle sighs of twilight's grace,
In the dark, we find our place.
Welcoming the dawn anew,
In this chill, our spirits grew.

Echoing Silence Beneath the Snow

Silent whispers through the trees,
Carried softly by the breeze.
Echoing where shadows dwell,
Tales of winter's icy spell.

Layers deep, the snow descends,
Wrapping earth, as time suspends.
In this hush, the world holds still,
Nature breathes, her voice a thrill.

Distant howls of wolves awake,
Breaking calm for solace's sake.
In the vastness, hearts unite,
Underneath the pale moonlight.

Gentle footprints mark the way,
Through the drifts where shadows play.
Every step, a story spun,
In the silence, we become one.

Deep within the heart of night,
Dreams take flight in frosted light.
As the stars begin to fade,
Echoes linger, soft and laid.

The Frost-Gleamed Pathways

Frozen pathways stretch afar,
Guiding souls beneath the star.
Each step leaves a silver trace,
In the quiet, lost in grace.

Whispers of the night enfold,
Stories written, dreams retold.
Frosty breath upon the air,
Leaves the world in a still stare.

Bridges spanning time and space,
In each corner, we embrace.
Upon the frost-gleamed ground we tread,
Mapping all the tales we've read.

As the moonlight starts to wane,
Journies merge, no hint of pain.
With our hearts, we find the way,
Through the night and into day.

Life shines bright on paths so cold,
Finding warmth in stories old.
Together, we will always roam,
In the frost, we find our home.

Dimly Lit Paths of Shattered Light

In shadows where the whispers creep,
Beneath a sky where secrets sleep.
The echoes dance on stony ground,
While silent fears begin to sound.

A flicker glows, a ghostly flare,
Leading hearts through the weighted air.
With every step, the darkness fights,
Yet still we tread on shattered lights.

Memories drift like autumn leaves,
Caught in webs that time deceives.
Each path we walk, a tale untold,
A journey carved in light and cold.

From hidden corners, visions rise,
Against the backdrop of twilight skies.
With trembling hands, we grasp our fate,
Embracing shadows we create.

Within the dim, our spirits soar,
Revealing truths we can't ignore.
As paths converge in fleeting night,
We find ourselves in shattered light.

A Frosty Reverie Unraveled

In dreams where frost begins to weave,
A tapestry of soft reprieve.
Each breath a cloud, each step a sigh,
A frozen world beneath the sky.

Whispers carried on the breeze,
Echoes hidden in the trees.
Crystals glisten like silver threads,
Mapping paths where silence spreads.

Upon the lake, a mirror shines,
Reflecting stars in thin designs.
The chill wraps round like velvet night,
In frosty dreams, we take our flight.

Yet time unravels like the lace,
As morning light begins to trace.
What once was still begins to move,
And frosty dreams begin to prove.

In reveries that gently fade,
The beauty lingers, unafraid.
Each moment crafted in the cold,
Holds memories that can't be sold.

Elysium of the Icy Veil

Beyond the veil where shadows creep,
Lies a realm, serene and deep.
Each flake of snow, a whispered prayer,
Floating softly in the air.

A world wrapped in a crystal quilt,
Each surface touched where silence built.
In frozen echoes, truth is found,
As dreams crystallize on hallowed ground.

Light dances through the frosted trees,
A symphony of winter's ease.
Each shimmer weaves a tale divine,
In this elysium, hearts entwine.

The icy breath of night does weave,
A narrative that bids us leave.
In depths of calm, we lose our way,
In this enigma we must stay.

Once lost, now found, in the divine,
Elysium beckons, a cosmic sign.
Wrapped in wonder, we must unveil,
The magic held in the icy veil.

Starlit Frost on a Shivering Night

The night unfolds with icy breath,
As stars above embrace the depth.
A blanket of frost on fields so wide,
Embraces dreams where shadows hide.

Crystals sparkle with a ghostly light,
Dancing softly in the quiet night.
Each twinkle tells of tales once spun,
Beneath the gaze of the watching sun.

Frost-laden whispers call out clear,
In the chill, our dreams draw near.
A shivering night, yet warmth will grow,
In starlit paths that weave and flow.

The sky, a canvas, dark and bright,
Holds secrets wrapped in pure delight.
As we wander through this serene plight,
We find ourselves in dreams of light.

Underneath a night so stark,
Hearts ignite, a whispered spark.
In the silence, love's gentle might,
Blooms forever in the starlit night.

Frosty Reflections in the Gloom

In the stillness of the night,
Shadows dance on icy ground.
Whispers echo soft and light,
Memories lost, yet profound.

Breath of winter, crisp and clear,
Frosty patterns grace the glass.
Silent stories, drawing near,
In the moment's fleeting pass.

Branches clad in frozen lace,
Nature's art, a haunting grace.
Glimmers twinkle, softly trace,
Beauty found in empty space.

Footsteps crunch beneath the star,
Every echo tells a tale.
Wanderers from near and far,
In the night, we gently sail.

Cold embrace, a sweet despair,
In the gloom, we find our peace.
Hearts connect, a bond laid bare,
In this frozen, still release.

Whispers of the Snowbound Heart

Amidst the silence, spirits sing,
Through the snow, love's whispers flow.
Gentle flurries, hearts take wing,
In the cold, our passions grow.

Frosted breath upon the air,
Softly gleaming, dreams take flight.
In the chill, we find our care,
Wrapped in warmth, we chase the light.

Snowflakes fall like tender sighs,
Painting landscapes, pure and white.
In their dance, a sweet reprise,
Filling hearts with sheer delight.

Beneath the moon's enchanting glow,
Whispers linger, softly heard.
In the quiet, love does grow,
Bound together by each word.

Through the frost, our steps entwine,
Two souls woven in the night.
In the snow, our hearts align,
As we bask in winter's light.

Night's Whisper in a Frozen World

In the darkness, secrets creep,
Winter's breath, a soft caress.
Moonlight dances, shadows leap,
Wrapping all in stillness, blessed.

Frozen branches bow and sway,
Echoes of a distant song.
In the night, we find our way,
Where the lost and dreamers long.

Every flake a tale to tell,
Whispers caught in frosty air.
In this world, we know it well,
Beauty hidden, lingered there.

Nights are silent, hearts awake,
Revealing truths that time forgot.
In the chill, we dare to take,
Paths that lead to what we sought.

As the night begins to fade,
We hold on to what's become.
In this frozen serenade,
Life embraces, softly hums.

Shining Traces of the Cold Moonlight

Underneath the silver glow,
Moonlight spills on snow-clad hills.
Whispers soft as breezes blow,
Calling forth the night's sweet thrills.

Every shadow, every gleam,
Draws us close to winter's heart.
In the whisper of a dream,
We traverse where lovers part.

Footsteps merging, paths align,
In the brilliance, sparks ignite.
Cold and warm, a sweet design,
Guided by the quiet light.

Silent moments shared in trust,
In the moon's embrace, we find.
Hearts entwined, as dreams adjust,
In the peace of night unkind.

Fleeting glances, treasured pause,
In the stillness, find our place.
Winter's chill, yet love's warm cause,
In the night's serene embrace.

Beneath the Shroud of Winter

The trees stand bare and still,
Their whispered secrets chill.
A blanket white, so deep,
Enfolds the land in sleep.

Beneath the frost, life waits,
In crystal coats, it waits.
The world a silent dream,
Wrapped in winter's gleam.

Footsteps crunch on icy ground,
In the stillness, peace is found.
Each breath a misty plume,
In nature's quiet room.

Stars twinkle in frosty skies,
While the moon softly sighs.
Night's tender, icy breath,
Carries whispers of death.

Yet hope stirs beneath the snow,
In the heart, life's ember glow.
Though winter claims its throne,
Spring will soon be known.

Subtle Gleams of Silent Nights

The moon casts a silver light,
Illuminating the night.
Stars flicker like distant dreams,
In silence, soft and serene.

Shadows dance with whispered grace,
In the calm, we find our place.
Gentle winds brush my face,
Nature's tender embrace.

Crickets sing their lullabies,
Beneath the vast, endless skies.
Each note a haunting refrain,
Echoes dance like soft rain.

The world held in tranquil slumber,
Each heartbeat a hopeful number.
Beneath the veil of the night,
Dreams take wing, taking flight.

In the stillness, hearts unite,
A tapestry woven tight.
Subtle gleams in the dark,
Ignite a tranquil spark.

The Frost on Forgotten Paths

Winding trails through ancient trees,
Whispers carried by the breeze.
Covered in a glistening frost,
Echoes of the past embossed.

Memories in the icy air,
Stories linger everywhere.
Footsteps traced in silver white,
Softly fade into the night.

Time stands still on these lost roads,
Where nature's beauty boldly glows.
Each step tells of life once known,
In the frost, the heart has grown.

Golden leaves lie curled and dry,
Beneath the sky where dreams can fly.
Frozen whispers of long ago,
Guide us gently through the snow.

Though paths may twist and times may change,
In the stillness, hearts remain.
The frost, a touch of sweet release,
Invites us to find our peace.

Snowflakes in the Dim Light

Snowflakes fall, a dance divine,
Each unique, a fleeting sign.
In the glow of streetlamp's hue,
They twirl like dreams, pure and true.

Blankets soft on rooftops lie,
Underneath the textured sky.
Whispers weave through winter's chill,
Frozen moments, time stands still.

Children laugh, their joy is bright,
Chasing shadows in the night.
Snowmen rise with carrot nose,
In this world where magic glows.

The quiet hum of evening peace,
Wraps us in sweet, soft release.
Footsteps crunch on frosted ground,
In this wonder, love is found.

So let the snowflakes gently fall,
A soft blanket over all.
In the dim light of the night,
We find warmth, our hearts ignite.

Winter's Ghosts in Moonlit Time

In the quiet night, shadows play,
Whispers of frost, where spirits sway.
Moonbeams dance upon the snow,
Echoes of dreams from long ago.

Branches heavy with a silver hue,
Silence speaks of the old and new.
Footprints linger, then fade away,
In winter's grip, the night holds sway.

Stars blink softly in deep repose,
A world transformed, as winter grows.
Time stands still, in the frozen air,
Ghosts of winter linger there.

Candles flicker, warmth inside,
While outside, icy winds abide.
The moon's soft glow, a guiding light,
Leading us through the long, dark night.

In whispers shared beneath the sky,
Winter's tales as time drifts by.
A magic spell, where dreams align,
In moonlit nights, our hearts entwine.

Chilled Whispers in a Hidden Grove

In a secret nook where silence reigns,
Chilled whispers float like gentle rains.
Frosty leaves beneath our feet,
Nature's breath, a soft retreat.

Twilight lingers, shadows creep,
The ancient trees, their secrets keep.
Every rustle tells a tale,
In the grove where spirits sail.

Moonlight weaves through branches bare,
A silken thread in the frosty air.
Dewdrops sparkle, diamonds found,
In this sanctuary, peace is crowned.

The breath of winter, crisp and pure,
Binds the heart with a calming lure.
In the stillness, time stands still,
Chilled whispers echo, gentle thrill.

A harmony of night's embrace,
Secluded moments, a sacred space.
Through the hush, our spirits rise,
In this grove, beneath the skies.

Frigid Reflections on a Glassy Lake

On a glassy lake, the world unfolds,
Frigid reflections, stories told.
Winter's mirror, still and wide,
Capturing dreams on nature's tide.

Silent ripples break the calm,
A haunting beauty, a soothing balm.
Frost-kissed shores, where whispers glide,
In frozen moments, time can bide.

The cobalt sky, a canvas vast,
Painting shades of winter's past.
Underneath, the depths conceal,
Secrets that the ice can feel.

Crisp air stirs with a chilly bite,
As twilight falls, embracing night.
Stars reflect like dreams awoken,
In this stillness, hearts are spoken.

Beneath the surface, life persists,
Frigid beauty in the mist.
In every shimmer, stories wake,
On this serene, glassy lake.

Dreamscapes in the Hushed Snowfall

In the hush of snowfall, dreams arise,
Blanketing earth under soft skies.
Whispers of white, tender and light,
Kissing the ground, a pure delight.

Snowflakes twirl like dancers free,
A magical realm for you and me.
Quiet moments drape the scene,
In dreamscapes where our hearts convene.

Footprints lead to places unknown,
In the stillness, we're never alone.
Each flake a story, a wish to share,
In the tender chill, a love laid bare.

Branches bow with a load of grace,
As winter weaves her soft embrace.
In the glowing light of twilight's call,
We find our joy in the hushed snowfall.

With every breath, a world transforms,
In the gentle silence, beauty warms.
Through dreamscapes bright, we drift away,
In the heart of winter, forever stay.

Enigmas Beneath the Snow

Beneath the snow, secrets sleep,
Whispers of the earth so deep.
Silent shadows softly play,
Veils of white where dreams decay.

Frosted branches, tales they weave,
Moonlit paths that none perceive.
In the stillness, magic stirs,
As the night its silence purrs.

Stars above, a distant glow,
Guiding thoughts through winter's flow.
Every flake a fleeting chance,
In the quiet, spirits dance.

Hushed are voices, time stands still,
Echoes linger, hearts can fill.
Nature hums a soft refrain,
As enigmas break the chain.

Awakening in morning light,
Secrets fade from endless night.
But in the chill, the mysteries grow,
Life reborn beneath the snow.

The Silence of Crystal Nights

Underneath the vast, dark sky,
Moonbeams twinkle, soft and shy.
Nights adorned in crystal grace,
Whispers float in quiet space.

Trees stand tall, their limbs aglow,
Covered in a frosty show.
Winds hold secrets, breathe them slow,
In the silence, heartbeats flow.

Stars above, like diamonds bright,
Guarding dreams through endless night.
Every twinkle, a silent prayer,
In the stillness, we all share.

Muffled sounds, a world confined,
Echoes lost, serenity defined.
Crystal nights, so pure and clear,
Hold our hopes, draw us near.

As dawn approaches, shadows fade,
In the light, the magic played.
Yet in memory, echoes stay,
Of crystal nights that slipped away.

Glistening Footprints on Ice

Footprints mark the frozen ground,
Stories told without a sound.
Each small step, a path we trace,
In the winter's cold embrace.

Glistening shards, the ice reflects,
Fragments of our past connects.
Hidden tales in every stride,
Moments lost, yet never hide.

Frigid air, a canvas white,
Painting memories in the night.
Through the chill, with hope we stride,
Finding warmth when worlds collide.

Nature watches, keeps her lore,
Silent guardian at the shore.
Each impression, fleeting grace,
In the stillness, find your place.

As the thaw begins to creep,
Footprints fade, but dreams don't sleep.
In every step, a truth we face,
On ice, we dance, we find our space.

Shimmering Lullabies of the Dark

In the dark, soft whispers sway,
Lullabies of night convey.
Stars above, they beckon near,
Singing songs for all to hear.

Moonlit paths in shadows play,
Guiding hearts that drift away.
Every hush a gentle touch,
Binding souls who crave so much.

Crickets chirp a soothing tune,
Beneath the watchful, silvery moon.
Nature's pulse, a beating heart,
In the quiet, we're a part.

Dreams take flight on midnight's breath,
Finding solace in the depth.
Shimmering lights and soft caress,
In the dark, we find our rest.

As night unfolds, we lose our fears,
Wrapped in dreams, our hearts in peers.
With every twinkle, hope ignites,
In shimmering lullabies of nights.

A Tapestry of Winter's Whimsy

Frosty breath on chilly air,
Dancing snowflakes play with care.
Whispers of a silver night,
Nature wrapped in pure delight.

Trees adorned in crystal frost,
Time stands still; no moment lost.
Footprints trace a story found,
In this wonderland unbound.

Children laugh as snowballs fly,
Joyful echoes fill the sky.
Winter's charm, a playful tease,
Hearts are warmed by memories.

In the twilight's gentle glow,
Shadows dance on hills below.
Moonlight weaves through branches bare,
Creating magic in the air.

As the night begins to fade,
Morning whispers, softly made.
Winter's whimsy, fleeting grace,
Leaves behind a timeless trace.

Twilight's Caress on the Snow

As the sun dips low and pale,
Twilight weaves a silver veil.
Snowflakes twinkle, dance, and spin,
Nature's beauty draws us in.

Crimson skies turn deep and blue,
Whispers of a night so true.
In this hush, the world feels right,
Wrapped in warmth, a cozy sight.

Footprints tell of paths once trod,
Silence falls like a soft nod.
Every flake, a fleeting kiss,
Moments held in frozen bliss.

Stars awaken, one by one,
Glistening like a million suns.
Nighttime's magic, soft and bright,
Cradling dreams in gentle light.

With each breath, a cloud appears,
Drawing near, we leave our fears.
Twilight's caress on the snow,
Brings a peace we long to know.

Glacial Echoes of the Heart

In the stillness, silence reigns,
Glacial echoes soothe our pains.
Heartbeats melt in winter's grip,
Nature's wisdom, a gentle sip.

Frozen streams of memory flow,
Carving paths where feelings grow.
Each crystal holds a whispered sigh,
Stories of the low and high.

Love's white blanket softly laid,
Drifting thoughts that never fade.
In this chill, our spirits soar,
Opening each forgotten door.

Snowflakes fall like tender dreams,
Merging hearts in silver beams.
Embers glow in the frosty air,
Warming souls that deeply care.

When the dawn begins to break,
Gentle light, a soft remake.
Glacial echoes linger sweet,
In the heart, a rhythmic beat.

Traces of Light in the Snow's Embrace

Sunlight kisses endless white,
Traces glow with pure delight.
Every step a silent song,
Nature's beauty, vast and strong.

Shadows dance on fields of gray,
Whispering as night meets day.
Fleeting moments wrapped in light,
Guiding hearts through softest night.

In the quiet, strength reveals,
Love's reflection softly heals.
Each heartbeat marked in snow so bright,
Tales of warmth in winter's light.

Footprints lead to memories dear,
Echoed laughter lightly near.
In this realm where shadows blend,
Hope and dreams ascend, transcend.

Beneath the stars, a promise glows,
Traces of love the cold wind knows.
In winter's depth, we find our place,
Embraced forever in its grace.

A Landscape of Ethereal Portraits

Brush strokes of light and shade,
Canvas dreams softly fade.
Mountains whisper, valleys sigh,
In colors that dance and fly.

Chasing shadows, time stands still,
In these frames, hearts they will.
Nature's secrets gently told,
In whispers of green and gold.

Underneath the azure skies,
A portrait of life softly lies.
Textures weave through every seam,
A tapestry born of a dream.

Birds take flight, paint the air,
Echoes of beauty everywhere.
Reflections in a tranquil stream,
Each glimpse becomes a fleeting dream.

Blossoms swirl in fragrant wind,
Stories of ages intertwined.
In this vast and vibrant lore,
A landscape forever to explore.

Whispers in the Winter Mist

In the hush of frosty air,
Whispers weave without a care.
Snowflakes dance on whispered sighs,
Nature's breath beneath pale skies.

Bare branches cradle dreams of white,
Stars blanket the silent night.
Footprints lost in frozen ground,
Echoes of the lost, profound.

Misty veils embrace the trees,
Frosted whispers, gentle breeze.
Time stands still, a moment's grace,
In winter's soft and sweet embrace.

Hark the call of distant dreams,
Wrapped in silver, soft moonbeams.
Night enfolds the world in peace,
Where worries fade, and sorrows cease.

Softly glowing from afar,
Hearts alight like a distant star.
In the mist, life's whispers weave,
A tapestry of hopes to believe.

Chilled Echoes of Dusk

As daylight wanes in soft refrain,
Chilled echoes of dusk remain.
Crickets sing their evening tunes,
Beneath the watchful, silvered moons.

Shadows stretch and nights ensue,
Casting dreams in twilight's hue.
Glistening stars begin to rise,
In the dance of darkened skies.

Whispers fill the chilly air,
Stories linger everywhere.
Silent night begins to weave,
Mysteries the heart believes.

In dusky shades, the world slows down,
Wrapping us in twilight's gown.
Every breath, a soft embrace,
In dusk's serene and tender space.

On the horizon, shadows play,
Marking the end of another day.
In the quiet, solace found,
In the chilled echoes all around.

Silvered Veils of Twilight

Underneath a sky aglow,
Silvered veils begin to flow.
Twilight dances, soft and slow,
In hues of lavender below.

Embers of day softly fade,
In twilight's magic, dreams are made.
Stars awaken, shy and bright,
As shadows curl with gentle light.

The world holds its breath in peace,
In this moment, all worries cease.
Moonlight spills its silken threads,
A cozy blanket, softly spreads.

Whispers of night start to creep,
In silvery silence, we gently sleep.
Crickets serenade the night,
Under stars that twinkle bright.

Awash in colors so divine,
Time slows down and hearts align.
In silvered veils, the dreams take flight,
Guided by the glow of twilight.

Luminous Silence of Frozen Streams

In winter's grasp, the waters freeze,
A shimmered hush beneath the trees.
Whispers of ice, a tranquil night,
Reflecting stars, a silver light.

Gentle sighs from branches sway,
As moonlight dances, soft and gray.
The world in slumber, deep and calm,
Wrapped in warmth, a night's sweet balm.

Echoes of peace in silent flow,
The frozen dreams begin to grow.
Luminous depths where shadows play,
In crystalline forms, they weave and sway.

Stillness carries a sacred tune,
Beneath the gaze of a watching moon.
Nature's breath held in timeless grace,
In frozen streams, we find our place.

The night whispers secrets, pure and true,
In the luminous quiet, thoughts renew.
A world transformed, in layers bright,
The beauty of darkness, kissed by light.

Secrets Held by Snowy Veils

Wrapped in white, a world so still,
Snowy veils on the quiet hill.
Each flake a whisper, soft and low,
Secrets of winter, we long to know.

Beneath the layers, stories sleep,
In the stillness, the earth will keep.
Hidden beneath, the life remains,
Bound in silence, like gentle chains.

The hush of snowflakes, sweet embrace,
Each one a memory, time cannot erase.
A silent promise of spring's return,
In icy cloaks, the embers burn.

The world transformed, a dreamlike sight,
Under the gaze of the starlit night.
Secrets guarded by the winter's breath,
Binding all life in cycles of death.

In the thaw, the whispers will rise,
Revealing truths beneath the skies.
But for now, in stillness we dwell,
With secrets kept by snowy veil.

Wraiths in the Winter Glade

In twilight's grace, the shadows play,
Wraiths wander in the glade's array.
Frozen figures in the soft mist,
Lost in wanderings, beneath the tryst.

They dance with whispers, wild and free,
Tracing the echoes of history.
The air is thick with stories old,
Of winter's magic, bold and cold.

In shimmering veils, their forms entwined,
Where frost meets breath, a world designed.
Each movement stirs the sleeping wood,
In frozen silence, where once they stood.

The moonlight casts a spectral glow,
As wraiths weave tales of long ago.
In every corner, shadows blend,
In this haunted space, time has no end.

A secret waltz beneath the stars,
Wrapped in memories, hidden scars.
In winter glades where dreams are spun,
The wraiths wander till night is done.

The Stillness of Crystal Air

In crystal air, the world holds breath,
A quiet pause, where time meets death.
Each shimmered leaf, a captured gleam,
In silence wrapped, as in a dream.

The frost embraces every space,
In stillness found, we find our grace.
Echoes linger in the snow,
Stories unfold, yet none will know.

With every gust, the chill inspires,
A dance of frost, as time expires.
The heart beats slow, the mind takes flight,
In crystal air, the soul finds light.

Amidst the still, a breath of peace,
In silent wonders, all fears cease.
For in the calm, we find our way,
In crystal air, we long to stay.

The world is hushed, and dreams emerge,
In winter's pause, we gently verge.
To find the essence, all laid bare,
In the stillness of the crystal air.

Shadows Cast by Winter's Grasp

In the pale light of the waning day,
Shadows stretch and twist at play,
Frosted breath in the evening air,
A silent world, a frosty prayer.

Trees stand tall in their silver coat,
Whispers echo, a lover's note,
Footprints linger in the snow,
Stories shared, but few will know.

Moonlight bathes the frozen ground,
Magic lingers, it spins around,
Each flake glimmers, a star kissed dream,
Nature's beauty, a perfect scheme.

As night falls, the chill encroaches,
A melody of silence approaches,
In winter's grasp, we find our peace,
As shadows dance and worries cease.

Hold this moment, let it last,
In the stillness, forget the past,
Embrace the chill, the night's soft light,
In winter's grasp, all feels right.

A Tapestry of Ice and Night

A tapestry woven with threads of ice,
Under the stars, oh, how they entice,
Glittering patterns in the moon's soft glow,
A beautiful portrait, nature's show.

Crystals dangle from branches bare,
Whispers of winter dance through the air,
Each breath released, a fleeting mist,
Moments of magic, too pure to resist.

Night cloaks the world in a silent wrap,
The winds hum softly, a lullaby map,
Under the blanket of the endless blue,
Dreams wander gently, spun from the true.

Stillness reigns where shadows reside,
A canvas of winter, so deep and wide,
Beneath the expanse, peace finds its way,
In the heart's quiet, forever to stay.

Each star a note in the night's sweet song,
A symphony of stillness where all belong,
A tapestry of ice, a wonderland bright,
In the peace of the dark, we greet the night.

Serene Chill of Dusk's Embrace

Dusk settles softly, a gentle sigh,
Whispers of twilight drift slowly by,
The horizon blushes, a tender hue,
Serene and calm, the world feels new.

Cool air dances, entwined with dreams,
Nature's night song, soft as it seems,
Stars begin winking, a playful tease,
Wrapped in the arms of a soothing breeze.

Shadows lengthen, as secrets unfold,
The heart grows warm while the air turns cold,
Night's gentle curtain begins to fall,
A moment of beauty that captivates all.

Under the canopy, peace takes flight,
In the serene chill of the approaching night,
Each breath a gift, a tender embrace,
Lost in the stillness, we find our place.

As twilight deepens, we linger near,
Together in silence, with nothing to fear,
The dusk invites thoughts that drift free,
In the embrace of the night, we just be.

The Crystalline Silence of Evening

Evening descends with a crystalline gleam,
A silence wraps round like a tender dream,
Stars flicker softly in the deepening blue,
A moment of beauty shared by the few.

The world slows down under night's tender care,
Each breath a whisper that dances in air,
Textures of twilight, so rich and profound,
In the stillness, peace is found.

Frosted whispers glide on the breeze,
Nature listens, suspended with ease,
Crisp echoes linger, a symphony sweet,
In evening's embrace, our hearts find their beat.

Gentle shadows play on the ground,
In the crystalline silence, joy can be found,
With each passing moment, stillness unfurls,
As twilight weaves magic in soft, gentle swirls.

The night wraps the earth in its cool, soft light,
Inviting dreams to take graceful flight,
In the crystalline silence, we pause and reflect,
Connected to all in this shared intellect.

The Chill of Lost Whispers

In the silence, shadows play,
Whispers lost along the way.
Echoes fade in softest night,
A memory, a fleeting sight.

Frosted breath in morning air,
Tales of old, too sweet to bear.
Voices linger, soft and low,
In the chill, the heart does know.

Trees stand bare against the grey,
Ghosts of laughter drift away.
Each sigh cradles warmth and cold,
A story waiting to be told.

Windswept secrets dance and weave,
In this twilight, few believe.
Yet in whispers, dreams still soar,
In the stillness, we explore.

Lost in thoughts that gently glide,
In the space where hopes abide.
The chill of whispers guides the way,
Through the night, into the day.

Resplendent Haze of Winter's Twilight

The twilight sky, a melting gold,
In winter's haze, the tales unfold.
Frosted whispers curl around,
As day fades softly to the ground.

Crimson clouds begin to swell,
In frozen light, all secrets dwell.
Nature dressed in silver lace,
Reflects the warmth of day's embrace.

Shadows stretch across the land,
Chasing dreams, both soft and grand.
The earth adorned in twilight's glow,
Glistening soft, a tranquil show.

With every breath, the silence speaks,
In winter's arms, the heart seeks.
A resplendent hush fills the space,
In this twilight, we find grace.

As stars ignite in velvet skies,
In the cold, our spirits rise.
Wrapped in layers, we wander free,
In winter's haze, eternally.

Icebound Visions of the Heart

Frozen streams and mirrored dreams,
In stillness, the heart redeems.
A canvas white, untouched, serene,
Where love's reflection becomes keen.

Icicles hang like crystal tears,
Whispering softly of our fears.
Yet in the chill, warmth softly glows,
A comfort only the heart knows.

Each heartbeat thumps in rhythmic flow,
Through winter's grasp, our spirits grow.
Visions dance upon the ice,
In every glance, a sacrifice.

Cloaked in frost, our dreams ignite,
Guided gently by the light.
In frozen depths, the soul takes flight,
With every spark, the heart feels bright.

Embraced by the cold, we learn to feel,
In visions bound, our hearts conceal.
Icebound dreams, forever cast,
In the silence, love holds fast.

The Subtle Art of Frozen Light

In whispers clear, the crystals shine,
Reflecting dreams, both yours and mine.
The world, a canvas painted white,
In the subtle art of frozen light.

Mist drifts gently, soft and slow,
Illuminating all below.
Every shadow holds a spark,
In the quiet, we embark.

Snowflakes grace the earth with care,
Each one holds a tale to share.
The fleeting moments, pure delight,
Captured in the wintry sight.

As daylight dims, the stars ignite,
Casting dreams in endless flight.
In this stillness, we ignite,
The subtle art of frozen light.

With every breath, we weave our tale,
On frosty winds, we set our sail.
In the beauty of the night,
We find peace in frozen light.

A Canvas of Crystal White

A blank page lies, so pure, so bright,
Whispers of winter, in soft twilight.
Light dances gently on frosted ground,
In silence, beauty's grace is found.

Trees stand tall, their branches lace,
In sparkling coats, they find their place.
Each flake a story, unique and rare,
Together they create a world so fair.

Footprints trace a path, soft and slow,
In this canvas, marred just so.
Moments captured in each breath,
The chill echoes life, not death.

Children laugh, their joy unleashed,
Snowballs fly, a playful feast.
Laughter carries on the breeze,
Through the wonder of winter trees.

As dusk descends, the shadows blend,
The day retreats, as colors bend.
A canvas painted, vast and wide,
In crystal white, our dreams abide.

An Elegy in the Icy Dusk

The twilight settles, cold and deep,
In icy arms, the world does sleep.
Shadows stretch, as day takes flight,
An elegy into the frozen night.

The wind does mourn, a haunting song,
Through empty streets, where we belong.
Each breath released, a foggy sigh,
In the stillness, memories lie.

Beneath the stars, a silver sheen,
Whispers of what once had been.
Echoes of laughter, now a ghost,
In this icy dusk, we linger most.

A lantern flickers, dimmed by frost,
In shadows, every warmth is lost.
Yet in this cold, we find our peace,
In the elegance of night's release.

As time flows on, we softly tread,
Among the echoes of words unsaid.
An elegy wraps, so soft, so just,
In icy dusk, we place our trust.

Shaded Paths Among the Glittering Snow

Among the trees, a path winds clear,
In glittering snow, the world draws near.
Footsteps whisper, secrets old,
In shaded realms, where stories unfold.

Sunlight sparkles, a diamond dance,
As shadows weave a soft romance.
Each turn reveals a sight anew,
In frosted wonders, the heart breaks through.

Branches bow, heavy with frost,
Nature's canvas, beauty embossed.
A chorus of silence sings so low,
On shaded paths, we gently go.

Every flake, a fleeting kiss,
In the hush, we find our bliss.
Time stands still, in this serene,
Peace in paths, where we have been.

With every step, our spirits soar,
In glittering snow, we long for more.
A dance of shadows and light's embrace,
Shaded paths, a lover's grace.

A Tale Woven in Frost

In the heart of night, a tale unfolds,
Woven in frost, with threads of gold.
Each crystal formed, a word of lore,
In frost-kissed whispers, we implore.

The moon casts light, a silver thread,
Guiding our dreams, where none have tread.
Through icy breath, our stories breathe,
In the quiet night, we find reprieve.

Nature listens, a patient ear,
To every secret we hold dear.
A tapestry blooms, both vast and tight,
In the chill of the soft, enchanting night.

Hearts unite in the winter's grip,
On this journey, we make our trip.
In every flake, a moment stays,
A tale woven, in myriad ways.

When dawn breaks soft, the frost will fade,
Yet tales of winter will never evade.
In our hearts, forever lost,
Each memory cherished, a life embossed.

The Frozen Dance of Twilight Specters

Upon the icy stage they glide,
Whispers of night, a spectral tide.
Veils of frost, with grace, they weave,
In stillness deep, the heart believes.

Twilight's glow begins to fade,
Shadows in a frozen parade.
Glimmers dance in a silent trance,
Echoes of a haunting chance.

In every swirl, a ghostly form,
In chilly air, a sudden storm.
With every twirl, the twilight sings,
The silent bells of winter rings.

Time stands still as they embrace,
Among the stars, they find their place.
The frozen winds, they carry dreams,
In winter's night, where magic gleams.

As dawn approaches, they retreat,
Leaving behind the cold, divine fleet.
Yet in the heart, their footsteps stay,
The frozen dance will not decay.

Beneath the Ice, Secrets Lie

Beneath the surface, shadows creep,
In icy depths where secrets sleep.
Whispers held in frozen breath,
Echoes of a long-lost death.

Crystals bound to stories old,
Tales of fortunes yet untold.
Silent depths, a time forgotten,
In every crack, the past is sown.

Underneath, the world shall keep,
Memories buried, buried deep.
Frozen tales of loss and gain,
In every layer, joy and pain.

As currents weave, they'll always bind,
What lies below, the heart shall find.
Drifting whispers, dreams comply,
In mysterious waters, secrets lie.

The icy cloak will thaw in time,
Revealing truths in perfect rhyme.
But for now, beneath the skies,
In silence still, the past's reprise.

A Serenade of Silent Shimmers

In moonlit nights, the waters glow,
A serenade, soft and slow.
Ripples dance with tender grace,
Embracing light in a calm embrace.

Each shimmer tells a tale untold,
Of mysteries wrapped in silver cold.
From depths unknown, music flows,
In every wave, a secret grows.

Stars come out to serenade,
While shadows play, in silence laid.
Harmonies of air and sea,
In quiet whispers, wild and free.

The nightingale sings its sweet refrain,
A melody of joy and pain.
Captured in the tranquil night,
The earth will hum, the heart takes flight.

As dawn appears, the song ebbs low,
Yet in our hearts, the echoes flow.
A serenade that won't forget,
The silent shimmers linger yet.

The Crystal Cloak of Dusk

A cloak of crystal drapes the sky,
As day departs, the stars float high.
In twilight's glow, the world ignites,
With hues that dance on endless nights.

Each star, a gem in dusk's embrace,
Illuminates the night's cool face.
The shadows stretch, the silence grows,
In the calm air where magic flows.

Beneath this cloak of fading light,
Dreams take flight into the night.
Whispers echo in soothing waves,
As twilight guards the paths it paves.

The world transforms in a gentle sigh,
As fleeting moments drift and fly.
In crystal hues, the evening's grace,
Captures time in a soft embrace.

As darkness falls, the beauty stays,
A crystal cloak in midnight's haze.
And in the quiet, hearts shall find,
The secrets held within the mind.

Whispers in the Winter

Silent flakes begin to fall,
A hush descends on all.
Breath of frost in the air,
Winter's spell, pure and rare.

Branches cloaked in shimmering white,
Stars twinkle with soft light.
Footsteps crunch on frozen ground,
In this quiet, peace is found.

Warmth beneath a knitted shawl,
Stories shared in evening's thrall.
Embers glow, the fire's embrace,
Frosty kisses, winter's grace.

Birds take flight in crisp blue skies,
Nature's wonders, endless sighs.
Whispers dance on icy streams,
Winter weaves its tender dreams.

As the moon begins to rise,
Glistening snow in tranquil guise.
Whispers echo, soft and clear,
In the winter, love is near.

Echoes of a Glacial Dawn

Morning breaks with gentle light,
Glaciers glimmer, pure and bright.
Whispers through the frosty air,
Nature's canvas, beyond compare.

Crisp and clear, the silence reigns,
Echoes of the melting chains.
Mountains wear their crowns of snow,
While the rivers gently flow.

Each breath held in the still,
Nature's secrets yet to spill.
Sunrise paints the icy scape,
A world that's forged in beauty's shape.

With every shard that catches rays,
A symphony of winter plays.
Glacial whispers start to bloom,
Dissolving shadows, banishing gloom.

As day unfolds with a golden hue,
Echoes beckon, pure and new.
In this moment, time stands still,
Awakening the heart to thrill.

Veil of Icy Dreams

Underneath the diamond stars,
Veil of dreams, forgotten scars.
With each breath, the cold bites deep,
A lullaby that sings us to sleep.

Crystals form on window panes,
Nature's art, with no refrains.
Time slows down in this embrace,
Within the veil, we find our place.

Footsteps lost in silver snow,
Paths of wonder, soft and slow.
Whispers linger, secrets shared,
In icy realms, we are ensnared.

Silhouettes of trees so bare,
Glimmers dancing in the air.
Silent dreams beneath the night,
Wrap us in this frosty light.

Veil of dreams, where spirits tread,
Countless stories left unsaid.
In the stillness, hearts unite,
In this realm of sheer delight.

Crystal Lace Beneath the Moon

Moonlight drapes the world in white,
Crystal lace, a pure delight.
Shimmers play on frozen streams,
Twinkling softly, sweetened dreams.

Frosty whispers in the night,
Stars align with silver light.
Nature pauses, takes a breath,
In this clear embrace of death.

Branches stretch like fingers long,
In the quiet, holds the song.
Echoes weave through icy air,
Cradling wishes, fragile, rare.

Underneath this tranquil sky,
Hearts take flight, we learn to fly.
In this magic, all is calm,
Wrapped in winter's gentle balm.

Crystal lace, a bed of snow,
Soft reflections, all aglow.
Beneath the moon, our dreams take flight,
In the stillness of the night.

Midnight's Glacial Embrace

The moon hangs low, a silver guide,
Whispers of frost where secrets hide.
Night drapes softly, a silken veil,
In shadows deep, the chill prevails.

Stars twinkle bright in the icy air,
Silent promises, a love laid bare.
Frozen branches, like hands outstretched,
Holding winter's dreams, forever etched.

The world asleep in a cold embrace,
Nature's beauty in tranquil grace.
Each breath a mist, a fleeting sigh,
Beneath the stretch of the endless sky.

Time stands still in this hallowed space,
Midnight's glacial touch we can't replace.
In togetherness, hearts beat slow,
Bound by the magic of ice and snow.

Awake in dreams where we both reside,
In midnight's embrace, we'll always bide.
Surrounded by peace, a stillness bright,
In glacial realms, we find our light.

Frosted Whispers of Abandon

Fields of white where memories flow,
Nature's hush is a soft, sweet woe.
Footsteps vanish, lost with the breeze,
In frost's gentle clutch, our hearts freeze.

Whispers of old linger in the night,
Secrets buried, hidden from sight.
The world feels heavy, a muted tone,
In every silence, I'm all alone.

Yet beauty dances with a chill in the air,
Silvered leaves falling without a care.
Winter's breath drapes a shroud of peace,
In frosted whispers, our worries cease.

A canvas painted in shades of grey,
As daylight fades, night claims the day.
In shadows deep where lost hopes lie,
Frosted echoes softly sigh.

In this quiet void, my heart remains,
Carried by winter's fragile chains.
In whispered breath, I find my way,
Through frosted paths, I'll gently sway.

Ghosts of Winter's Lullaby

Beneath the quilt of a starry night,
Ghosts of winter take their flight.
Carried softly on whispers rare,
Their presence dances in frosty air.

Hushed lullabies of the frosted land,
Echo in corners where we once stood hand in hand.
Memories buried beneath tracks of snow,
Resurface gently in the moon's soft glow.

Shadows creep where the cold winds wail,
Tales of longing in the winter's tale.
In every flake, a story's begun,
Haunting melodies from the frozen sun.

Ghosts of laughter linger and sway,
Binding the night with their gentle play.
In the quiet hush, they softly sigh,
Lullabies whispering, never to die.

Through the snow and frost, their spirits glide,
In the silent night, they'll always bide.
With every breath, their echoes remain,
Ghosts of winter, a love unchained.

Shadowy Gleams of the Frozen World

In a frozen realm where shadows dwell,
Gleams of light weave their silent spell.
Crystals shimmering on the frosty ground,
A beauty hidden, waiting to be found.

Amidst the hush, soft creatures roam,
Nature's whispers creating a home.
Each step a treasure, each breath a song,
In this land of frost, we all belong.

The sky dons a cloak of deep midnight blue,
Painting the world in dreams anew.
Shadows flutter like wings of despair,
Yet gleams of hope linger in the air.

Silent forests where secrets are kept,
In this quiet world, memories are swept.
With every heartbeat, shadows intertwine,
In frozen beauty, our souls align.

A journey ventured through winter's embrace,
Finding our way in this timeless space.
In shadowy gleams, we dance and twirl,
In harmony's grace, the frozen world.

Milton Keynes UK
Ingram Content Group UK Ltd.
UKHW010228111224
452348UK00011B/598